*For Savannah,
Have fun with Freddy Fr*

Freddy Frog and the Forgotten Birthday

A Tale from Ferndale
Story and Illustrations by Ree Gillett

Order this book online at www.trafford.com
or email orders@trafford.com

Most Trafford titles are also available at major online book retailers.

© Copyright 2013, 2014 Ree Gillett.

All rights reserved. No part of this publication may be reproduced, stored in a retrieval system, or transmitted, in any form or by any means, electronic, mechanical, photocopying, recording, or otherwise, without the written prior permission of the author.

Printed in the United States of America.

ISBN: 978-1-4907-1873-6 (sc)
978-1-4907-1874-3 (e)

Library of Congress Control Number: 2013920694

Because of the dynamic nature of the Internet, any web addresses or links contained in this book may have changed since publication and may no longer be valid. The views expressed in this work are solely those of the author and do not necessarily reflect the views of the publisher, and the publisher hereby disclaims any responsibility for them.

Any people depicted in stock imagery provided by Thinkstock are models, and such images are being used for illustrative purposes only.
Certain stock imagery © Thinkstock.

Trafford rev. 02/07/2014

 www.trafford.com

North America & international
toll-free: 1 888 232 4444 (USA & Canada)
fax: 812 355 4082

For Anni, Mike and Natasha

And for Neil

Thank you, one and all!

Freddy Frog woke up and stretched his long green arms. He yawned and was just about to go back to sleep when he remembered that today was special!

It was his birthday!

He sat up in bed with butterflies dancing in his stomach.

Every year his friends left him surprise presents!

He looked around the room . . . no presents.

He looked on the shelf . . . no presents.

He looked on his bedside table . . . no presents.

Freddy Frog crawled out of bed, had a few flies for breakfast and tossed his pyjamas onto the chair.

Then he left for a long, sad walk over the hills, feeling very sorry for himself.

Meanwhile, on the other side of Ferndale, Hailey Hedgehog sat knitting. She looked out the window and spotted a flash of green.

"What is Freddy Frog doing stomping away over the hill? He looks very grumpy!" Hailey said to herself.

And then she remembered! Today was Freddy Frog's birthday! She had totally forgotten!

Something had to be done, and quickly, before he returned!

She charged out the door and down the hill, as fast as she could, to the tree where Chester Chipmunk lived.

She giggled as she remembered the gift that she had given Freddy Frog the year before. She had knitted him a beautiful woolen hat but it came right down over his eyes.

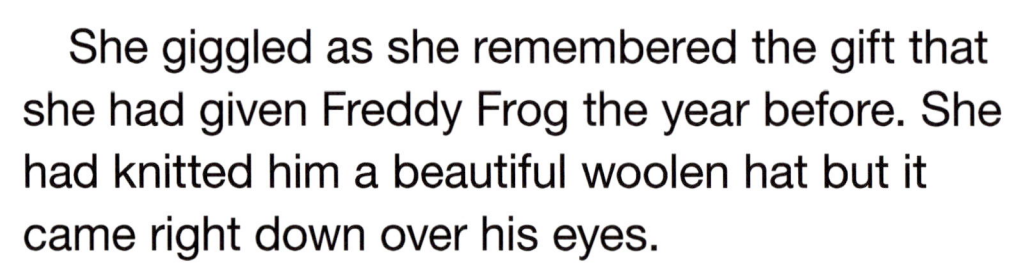

"Anyone home?" Hailey called as she knocked on the door.

Chester Chipmunk opened the door almost the minute she started knocking!

"Come in, come in!" he said with a smile. "I was just going to have a cup of acorn tea."

Hailey wasn't sure there was time, but she loved acorn tea.

"I would love some tea," she said.

"His birthday? Oh no! I forgot too! Last year I gave him a special acorn, but he didn't know what to do with it! What can we do?" Chester asked.

"Let's go ask Max the Mole," Hailey suggested.

As they came out of Chester's tree they could see Freddy Frog walking away, with his head down.

They ran as fast as they could up to Max's home on the hill.

"Max! Max!" They shouted down into the dark hole. They heard a little shuffling noise below and then it was quiet.

"Max!" They shouted again a bit louder.

The shuffling got closer and closer.

Finally Max the Mole popped his head up out of the hole. He blinked his eyes in the bright sunlight.

"What is going on up here? What is all this ruckus?"

"It's Freddy Frog's birthday today!" The two friends shouted together.

Max bounced right up and out of his hole.

"Oh, it is, is it? I'd completely forgotten! I don't have a present for him."

"We don't either," said Chester and they both told him about their presents the year before.

"Well, I gave Freddy Frog a nice, juicy worm, the best I could find, but he doesn't like worms!" Max told them. "In fact, you should have seen his face! He did say thank you, but I don't think he ate it."

Hailey was getting nervous. Freddy Frog might come back any minute!

"Hurry up! He'll be back soon," she warned them.

"He might like a book about frogs," Max proposed.

"Nice idea, but he already has a lot of books about frogs," Chester responded.

"A fly swatter?" Hailey suggested.

"No, he can catch them with his tongue," Chester said.

They thought for a very long time.

"A party!" Chester Chipmunk finally shouted.

"Yes!" Hailey and Max chimed in.

"Hurry!" they all shouted at the same time. "Let's have the party by the brook in front of Chester's tree!"

Down they ran to the brook, as fast as their legs could take them.

Max decorated around the tree with beautiful fuchsia flowers tied up like lanterns. Hailey made a delicious acorn cake with crunchy flies sprinkled on it and Chester set the table with his favorite acorn tops for plates.

It was looking quite festive and cheery and Hailey was just taking the cake out of the oven. They were almost ready!

Suddenly they heard a splash from the brook.

The three little mice had been busy gathering branches, acorns and stones for a special gift. They were working very hard. Two of them passed a branch to the third mouse to try and fill in the gap when:

"Oh no!" The little mouse lost his balance

and fell right into the rushing water!

"Help!" he cried.

The two mice on the rock tried to pull their friend out.

But it was wet and slippery and they slid right down into the brook with their little friend.

They were traveling downstream at a fast pace, bobbing up and down in the water.

Luckily, a small branch was also floating along and they managed to scramble up on top of it and only just in time! They were very tired and couldn't swim very well.

Chester ran down to the water, grabbed the mice and pulled them out to safety!

What had they been doing?

Max the Mole knew exactly what they had been up to!

With a little help from the mice, Max pushed a big stone into place and the dam was finished! They worked hard to fill in all the little spaces where water could get through.

And the pond started to fill up.

And while his friends were getting a special birthday ready for him, Freddy Frog had been walking up and down the hills thinking.

He started off feeling very grumpy because he hadn't seen any presents from his friends.

Then he remembered his gifts from the year before; Hailey's knitted hat that had covered his eyes, Chester's acorn that he didn't know what to do with and finally, Mole's big, fat worm that was nowhere near as delicious as crunchy flies.

A smile began to tug at the corners of Freddy Frog's mouth and he began to chuckle.

"The best gift ever," Freddy Frog thought to himself. "is to be with my friends." And he thought this lovely thought just as he came over the hill and saw his friends by the river, busily working together on something.

"Hi, my good friends!" he called out as he started down towards them.

He was so happy to see them that he ran all the way down the hill.

"HAPPY BIRTHDAY!!!!"

His friends shouted back to him. They all noticed he was wearing a smile a mile wide!

And the festivities began. The Birthday Frog floated happily in his new pond. He just loved those mice. What a wonderful idea!

They played Blind Man's Bluff and Mole was the winner every time. He was used to not seeing and using his ears instead to find things.

Chester Chipmunk showed Hailey how to play Toss the Acorn.

"Time for the cake," Hailey shouted as she brought out the birthday cake from Chester´s home in the tree.

And he huffed and he puffed and he blew out all the candles.

Everyone clapped for joy and gobbled up every last crumb, even the crunchy flies on top.

Later that night, when Freddy crawled into bed, he thought it was probably one of the best birthdays ever!

The paintings on the walls in Hailey Hedgehog's and Chester Chipmunk's houses are painted in the style of two very famous painters.

Giuseppe Arcimboldo lived 500 years ago in Italy. He painted portraits using objects from nature like leaves and branches and seeds. Chester Chipmunk tried to create a portrait of himself in the same style.

Try making a picture of yourself using leaves and fruit. It's fun!

Vincent van Gogh was born in Holland in 1853 and lived in France. Now he is very famous, although when he was alive he struggled and was poor during most of his life. He only sold one painting and only had one ear due to a crazy moment when he actually cut the other one off.

His paintings were full of bright colors and bold lines.

His painting, "Sunflowers" is famous. In Hailey's picture, we have snuck little hedgehogs in as the flowers. I'm sure you know what it should really look like!

Lightning Source UK Ltd.
Milton Keynes UK
UKIC01n2242080414
229622UK00009B/71